EMMANUEL JOSEPH

Blockchain and Beyond: Exploring Cryptocurrency Trade

Copyright © 2025 by Emmanuel Joseph

All rights reserved. No part of this publication may be reproduced, stored or transmitted in any form or by any means, electronic, mechanical, photocopying, recording, scanning, or otherwise without written permission from the publisher. It is illegal to copy this book, post it to a website, or distribute it by any other means without permission.

First edition

This book was professionally typeset on Reedsy.
Find out more at reedsy.com

Contents

1. Chapter 1 — 1
2. Chapter 7: Cryptocurrency Trading Strategies — 7
3. Chapter 8: Security Measures in Cryptocurrency Trading — 9
4. Chapter 9: The Impact of Blockchain on Industries — 11
5. Chapter 10: Environmental Impact of Blockchain Technology — 13
6. Chapter 11: Future Trends in Blockchain and Cryptocurrency — 15
7. Chapter 12: Embracing the Blockchain Revolution — 18

1

Chapter 1

Chapter 1: The Birth of Blockchain Technology In the last decade, blockchain technology has transformed from an obscure concept into a foundational pillar of the modern digital economy. Introduced through the enigmatic Satoshi Nakamoto's Bitcoin white paper in 2008, blockchain technology offered a new paradigm for decentralized, transparent, and secure data management. Unlike traditional centralized databases, a blockchain is a distributed ledger maintained by a network of nodes, ensuring data integrity through cryptographic validation.

The revolutionary idea of blockchain lies in its ability to create trust in a trustless environment. Each transaction added to the blockchain is verified by a consensus mechanism, such as Proof of Work or Proof of Stake, ensuring that malicious actors cannot easily manipulate the data. This innovation has profound implications, not only for financial transactions but for any scenario where secure and transparent record-keeping is critical.

Blockchain's initial application, Bitcoin, demonstrated the potential of digital currencies to operate independently of traditional financial institutions. Bitcoin's decentralized nature and limited supply made it an attractive alternative to fiat currencies, especially in regions with unstable economies. As the technology matured, a myriad of other cryptocurrencies and blockchain-based applications emerged, each aiming to address specific use cases and improve upon Bitcoin's limitations.

Despite its disruptive potential, blockchain technology faces several challenges. Scalability, energy consumption, and regulatory concerns are among the most pressing issues. As the technology evolves, developers and policymakers must collaborate to address these challenges and unlock blockchain's full potential, ensuring that its benefits are accessible to all.

Chapter 2: The Evolution of Cryptocurrencies In the aftermath of Bitcoin's success, a plethora of new cryptocurrencies emerged, each with unique features and purposes. Ethereum, introduced by Vitalik Buterin in 2015, expanded the scope of blockchain technology by enabling programmable smart contracts. These self-executing contracts automate complex transactions and agreements, paving the way for decentralized applications (dApps) and the burgeoning decentralized finance (DeFi) ecosystem.

The rise of cryptocurrencies also led to the development of privacy-focused coins, such as Monero and Zcash. These cryptocurrencies prioritize user anonymity by employing advanced cryptographic techniques, making it difficult to trace transactions. While privacy coins have garnered significant interest from individuals seeking enhanced financial privacy, they have also attracted scrutiny from regulators concerned about their potential misuse for illicit activities.

Another notable development in the cryptocurrency landscape is the proliferation of stablecoins. These digital assets are pegged to traditional fiat currencies or other stable assets, offering the benefits of cryptocurrencies without the volatility. Stablecoins have become a popular medium for trading and transferring value, particularly in regions with limited access to traditional banking services.

The cryptocurrency market is constantly evolving, driven by innovation and the quest for improved security, scalability, and usability. As new projects and technologies emerge, the landscape will continue to shift, presenting both opportunities and challenges for investors, developers, and regulators.

Chapter 3: Decentralized Finance (DeFi) Decentralized Finance, or DeFi, is a rapidly growing sector within the blockchain ecosystem that aims to recreate traditional financial services in a decentralized manner. By leveraging smart contracts and blockchain technology, DeFi projects offer a wide range of financial services, including lending, borrowing, trading, and yield farming, without the need for intermediaries such as banks or brokers.

DeFi's appeal lies in its ability to provide financial services to anyone with an internet connection, regardless of their location or socio-economic status. This democratization of finance has the potential to empower individuals and communities that have been historically underserved by traditional financial institutions. Furthermore, DeFi protocols are typically open-source, fostering innovation and collaboration within the community.

One of the most significant innovations in the DeFi space is the concept of automated market makers (AMMs). AMMs, such as Uniswap and Balancer, use algorithms to facilitate trading between users, eliminating the need for order books and centralized exchanges. This innovation has led to increased liquidity and reduced trading fees, making it easier for users to participate in the cryptocurrency market.

Despite its promise, DeFi is not without risks. Smart contract vulnerabilities, regulatory uncertainty, and the potential for market manipulation are among the challenges that must be addressed. As the DeFi ecosystem matures, it will be crucial for developers, auditors, and regulators to work together to ensure the security and stability of these decentralized financial platforms.

Chapter 4: The Rise of Non-Fungible Tokens (NFTs) Non-fungible tokens, or NFTs, have taken the world by storm, revolutionizing the way we perceive and interact with digital assets. Unlike cryptocurrencies, which are fungible and interchangeable, NFTs represent unique digital assets that cannot be replicated or exchanged on a one-to-one basis. This uniqueness makes NFTs ideal for representing digital art, collectibles, and other one-of-a-kind items.

The NFT craze began in earnest with the success of projects like CryptoKitties, which allowed users to buy, sell, and breed digital cats. Since then, the NFT market has exploded, with artists, musicians, and creators of all kinds embracing the technology to monetize their work. High-profile sales, such as Beeple's $69 million digital artwork auction at Christie's, have garnered significant attention and fueled the growth of the NFT ecosystem.

NFTs also have potential applications beyond the art world. They can be used to tokenize real-world assets, such as real estate, intellectual property, and even concert tickets, enabling new forms of ownership and transfer. Additionally, NFTs can be integrated with virtual worlds and gaming platforms, allowing users to own and trade in-game assets across different environments.

As with any emerging technology, NFTs come with their own set of challenges. Environmental concerns, copyright issues, and market speculation are among the factors that need to be addressed for the sustainable growth of the NFT space. By fostering a culture of responsible innovation and collaboration, the NFT community can continue to explore new possibilities and expand the boundaries of digital ownership.

Chapter 5: Regulatory Landscape and Compliance The rapid growth of the cryptocurrency and blockchain industry has attracted the attention of regulators worldwide. As governments grapple with the implications of these technologies, the regulatory landscape is constantly evolving. Different jurisdictions have adopted varying approaches to regulating cryptocurrencies, ranging from outright bans to more progressive frameworks that encourage innovation while ensuring consumer protection and financial stability.

In the United States, regulatory agencies such as the Securities and Exchange Commission (SEC) and the Commodity Futures Trading Commission (CFTC) have taken an active role in overseeing the cryptocurrency market. The SEC has focused on determining whether certain cryptocurrencies qualify as securities, while the CFTC has been more concerned with regulating cryptocurrency derivatives and futures markets. Additionally, the Financial Crimes Enforcement Network (FinCEN) has implemented anti-money laundering (AML) and know-your-customer (KYC) requirements for cryptocurrency businesses.

The European Union has also been proactive in developing a comprehensive regulatory framework for cryptocurrencies and blockchain technology. The proposed Markets in Crypto-Assets (MiCA) regulation aims to create a harmonized legal framework across member states, addressing issues such as consumer protection, market integrity, and financial stability. MiCA also includes provisions for stablecoins and decentralized finance, reflecting the

EU's commitment to fostering innovation while mitigating risks.

Other countries, such as China and India, have taken a more restrictive approach to cryptocurrency regulation. In China, the government has implemented a series of measures to clamp down on cryptocurrency trading and mining, citing concerns about financial stability and environmental impact. India, meanwhile, has been considering a ban on private cryptocurrencies, while exploring the potential of a central bank digital currency (CBDC).

As the cryptocurrency industry continues to evolve, regulatory clarity and compliance will be essential for its sustainable growth. By engaging with regulators and adhering to established guidelines, industry participants can help shape a regulatory environment that balances innovation with the need for consumer protection and market stability.

Chapter 6: The Role of Central Bank Digital Currencies (CBDCs)
Central Bank Digital Currencies (CBDCs) have emerged as a significant area of interest for central banks worldwide. These digital currencies, issued and regulated by central banks, aim to provide the benefits of cryptocurrencies while maintaining the stability and trust associated with traditional fiat currencies. CBDCs have the potential to transform the global financial system, enhancing payment efficiency, reducing transaction costs, and promoting financial inclusion.

One of the primary motivations for developing CBDCs is the declining use of physical cash in many countries. As digital payments become increasingly popular, central banks seek to ensure that their monetary policy tools remain effective and that the public has access to a safe and reliable means of payment. Additionally, CBDCs can help central banks address challenges such as money laundering, tax evasion, and the proliferation of private cryptocurrencies.

Several countries have already made significant progress in developing and piloting CBDCs. China's digital yuan, also known as the Digital Currency Electronic Payment (DCEP), is one of the most advanced CBDC projects globally. The People's Bank of China has conducted extensive trials of the digital yuan in various cities, exploring its potential use cases and gathering valuable insights for its eventual nationwide rollout.

In Europe, the European Central Bank (ECB) has been actively researching the potential benefits and risks of a digital euro. The ECB aims to ensure that the digital euro complements existing payment systems and enhances the efficiency of cross-border transactions. Similarly, the Bank of England has been exploring the feasibility of a digital pound, focusing on issues such as privacy, security, and financial stability.

Despite the growing interest in CBDCs, their implementation poses several challenges. Ensuring the security and privacy of digital currencies, maintaining the stability of the financial system, and addressing potential disintermediation of commercial banks are among the critical concerns that central banks must address. As CBDC initiatives progress, collaboration between central banks, policymakers, and technology providers will be essential to navigate these challenges and unlock the full potential of digital currencies.

2

Chapter 7: Cryptocurrency Trading Strategies

Cryptocurrency trading has become increasingly popular as more individuals and institutions seek to capitalize on the volatile nature of digital assets. Trading strategies in the cryptocurrency market vary widely, ranging from short-term speculative trades to long-term investment approaches. Understanding these strategies can help traders navigate the market more effectively and make informed decisions.

One common trading strategy is day trading, which involves buying and selling cryptocurrencies within the same day to take advantage of short-term price movements. Day traders rely on technical analysis, using charts and indicators to identify patterns and trends. They often employ strategies such as scalping, which involves making numerous small trades to capture minor price fluctuations, and momentum trading, which focuses on assets experiencing strong upward or downward trends.

Swing trading is another popular strategy, where traders aim to capture price swings over several days or weeks. Swing traders use a combination of technical and fundamental analysis to identify potential entry and exit points. They look for assets that show signs of reversal or continuation of existing trends and make trades based on these predictions.

For those with a longer-term perspective, hodling (a play on the word "hold") is a strategy where investors buy and hold onto cryptocurrencies for an extended period, regardless of short-term market fluctuations. This approach is based on the belief that the value of cryptocurrencies will increase over time due to their limited supply and growing adoption. Hodlers often focus on well-established cryptocurrencies, such as Bitcoin and Ethereum, which have a proven track record and a strong community of supporters.

Arbitrage is another strategy that involves taking advantage of price differences between different exchanges. Arbitrage traders buy an asset on one exchange where the price is lower and sell it on another exchange where the price is higher, pocketing the difference. This strategy requires quick execution and a keen eye for market inefficiencies, as price discrepancies can disappear rapidly.

While these trading strategies offer potential opportunities for profit, they also come with risks. The cryptocurrency market is highly volatile and can be influenced by various factors, including regulatory developments, technological advancements, and market sentiment. Traders must be prepared to manage these risks and develop a disciplined approach to trading to succeed in the long run.

3

Chapter 8: Security Measures in Cryptocurrency Trading

Security is a paramount concern in the world of cryptocurrency trading, as the decentralized nature of digital assets presents unique challenges and risks. Ensuring the safety of one's funds and personal information is crucial for any trader or investor. By implementing robust security measures, individuals can protect themselves from potential threats and vulnerabilities.

One of the most critical aspects of securing cryptocurrency assets is the use of hardware wallets. Unlike software wallets, which are connected to the internet and therefore more susceptible to hacking, hardware wallets store private keys offline. This makes it significantly more difficult for malicious actors to gain access to the funds. Popular hardware wallets, such as Ledger and Trezor, provide an added layer of security through features like PIN codes and recovery seed phrases.

In addition to using hardware wallets, traders should also employ strong, unique passwords for their exchange accounts and enable two-factor authentication (2FA). 2FA adds an extra layer of protection by requiring users to provide a second form of verification, such as a code sent to their mobile device, in addition to their password. This makes it more challenging for attackers to gain unauthorized access to accounts.

Regularly updating software and firmware is another essential security practice. Developers frequently release updates to address vulnerabilities and improve security. Keeping wallets, exchange accounts, and other related software up to date can help prevent potential exploits and attacks.

Phishing attacks are a common threat in the cryptocurrency space, where attackers attempt to trick individuals into revealing sensitive information, such as private keys or login credentials. To avoid falling victim to phishing, traders should exercise caution when clicking on links or downloading attachments from unknown sources. It's also essential to verify the authenticity of websites and services before entering any personal information.

Lastly, diversifying one's holdings across multiple wallets and exchanges can help mitigate the risk of losing all assets in the event of a security breach. By spreading funds across different platforms, traders can reduce their exposure to potential threats and ensure that their investments are better protected.

4

Chapter 9: The Impact of Blockchain on Industries

Blockchain technology extends far beyond the realm of cryptocurrencies, with the potential to revolutionize various industries by providing enhanced security, transparency, and efficiency. As organizations explore the possibilities of blockchain, its applications continue to expand, transforming traditional processes and creating new opportunities.

In the financial sector, blockchain has the potential to streamline processes, reduce costs, and enhance security. Traditional financial transactions often involve multiple intermediaries, which can lead to delays and increased fees. Blockchain technology enables direct peer-to-peer transactions, eliminating the need for intermediaries and reducing the time and cost associated with transferring funds. Additionally, blockchain's immutable nature ensures that transaction records are secure and transparent, reducing the risk of fraud and enhancing trust.

Supply chain management is another industry poised for disruption by blockchain technology. By providing a transparent and tamper-proof record of the entire supply chain, blockchain can help organizations track the movement of goods, verify the authenticity of products, and ensure compliance with regulations. This increased visibility can lead to improved efficiency, reduced counterfeiting, and enhanced trust between supply chain partners.

The healthcare industry can also benefit from blockchain technology, particularly in the areas of data management and patient privacy. Blockchain's decentralized nature allows for secure and transparent storage of medical records, ensuring that patients have control over their data and that it can only be accessed by authorized parties. This can lead to improved interoperability between healthcare providers, enhanced patient privacy, and more efficient sharing of medical information.

Blockchain technology also has potential applications in the energy sector, particularly in the management of decentralized energy grids and peer-to-peer energy trading. By enabling secure and transparent transactions between energy producers and consumers, blockchain can facilitate the efficient distribution of energy and reduce reliance on centralized power companies. This can lead to a more sustainable and resilient energy infrastructure.

As blockchain technology continues to evolve, its potential applications across various industries are becoming increasingly apparent. By embracing this technology, organizations can unlock new efficiencies, enhance security, and drive innovation, ultimately transforming the way we live and work.

5

Chapter 10: Environmental Impact of Blockchain Technology

As blockchain technology and cryptocurrencies gain widespread adoption, concerns about their environmental impact have come to the forefront. The energy consumption associated with certain blockchain networks, particularly those using Proof of Work (PoW) consensus mechanisms, has raised questions about the sustainability of these technologies. Addressing these environmental challenges is crucial for the long-term viability of blockchain and cryptocurrency ecosystems.

Proof of Work, the consensus mechanism used by Bitcoin and several other cryptocurrencies, relies on a process called mining. Miners compete to solve complex mathematical puzzles, which requires significant computational power and energy consumption. This process secures the network and validates transactions, but it also results in a substantial carbon footprint. As the popularity of cryptocurrencies has grown, so has the environmental impact of mining operations, leading to increased scrutiny from environmental advocates and policymakers.

In response to these concerns, several initiatives are underway to reduce the environmental impact of blockchain technology. One approach is the development and adoption of alternative consensus mechanisms, such as Proof of Stake (PoS). Unlike PoW, PoS does not require energy-intensive computations. Instead, validators are chosen to create new blocks and validate transactions based on the number of coins they hold and are willing to "stake" as collateral. This approach significantly reduces energy consumption while maintaining network security and decentralization.

Another strategy to address the environmental impact of blockchain technology is the use of renewable energy sources for mining operations. Some mining companies are exploring the use of solar, wind, and hydroelectric power to reduce their carbon footprint. By harnessing renewable energy, these operations can mitigate the environmental impact of mining and contribute to a more sustainable blockchain ecosystem.

In addition to these technological and operational changes, there is a growing emphasis on the role of blockchain in promoting environmental sustainability. Blockchain-based projects are being developed to address various environmental challenges, such as carbon trading, supply chain transparency, and conservation efforts. By leveraging blockchain's transparency and immutability, these projects aim to create more efficient and accountable systems for managing environmental resources.

As the blockchain and cryptocurrency industries continue to evolve, addressing their environmental impact will be essential for their long-term success. By embracing sustainable practices and innovative technologies, the community can work towards a more environmentally responsible future.

6

Chapter 11: Future Trends in Blockchain and Cryptocurrency

The future of blockchain technology and cryptocurrencies is filled with exciting possibilities and potential challenges. As the industry continues to mature, several trends are likely to shape its development and impact on the global economy.

One significant trend is the increasing integration of blockchain technology with other emerging technologies, such as artificial intelligence (AI), the Internet of Things (IoT), and 5G. The convergence of these technologies can create new opportunities for innovation and efficiency across various industries. For example, blockchain can provide secure and transparent data management for AI algorithms, while IoT devices can benefit from blockchain's decentralized architecture to enhance security and interoperability.

Another trend is the growing interest in decentralized autonomous organizations (DAOs). DAOs are organizations governed by smart contracts and run by their members, without the need for centralized leadership. By leveraging blockchain technology, DAOs can enable more democratic and transparent decision-making processes, allowing stakeholders to have a direct say in the organization's operations. This trend has the potential to transform traditional organizational structures and empower individuals to take a more active role in governance.

Interoperability between different blockchain networks is also expected to become increasingly important. As the number of blockchain platforms and applications continues to grow, the ability to seamlessly transfer assets and data between different networks will be crucial. Projects like Polkadot and Cosmos are working to create interoperability solutions that enable different blockchains to communicate and interact with one another, fostering a more connected and efficient ecosystem.

Regulatory developments will continue to play a significant role in shaping the future of blockchain and cryptocurrencies. As governments around the world develop and implement new regulations, the industry will need to adapt to ensure compliance and maintain growth. Clear and consistent regulatory frameworks can provide the necessary guidance for businesses and investors can thrive within a regulated environment. Additionally, international cooperation on regulatory standards will be essential to address cross-border challenges and promote the widespread adoption of blockchain technology.

Another area of growth is the development of central bank digital currencies (CBDCs). As discussed earlier, CBDCs have the potential to reshape the financial landscape by providing a secure and efficient means of digital payment. Central banks around the world are actively researching and piloting CBDC projects, and their successful implementation could lead to increased trust and acceptance of digital currencies on a global scale.

The rise of tokenization is another trend that will likely shape the future of blockchain and cryptocurrencies. Tokenization involves representing real-world assets, such as real estate, commodities, or intellectual property, as digital tokens on a blockchain. This process can enhance liquidity, reduce transaction costs, and enable fractional ownership, making it easier for individuals and businesses to invest in and trade various assets.

As blockchain technology continues to evolve, the focus on scalability and interoperability will be crucial for its success. Layer 2 solutions, such as the Lightning Network for Bitcoin and various Ethereum scaling projects, aim to increase transaction throughput and reduce fees, making blockchain networks more efficient and accessible. Additionally, projects that

CHAPTER 11: FUTURE TRENDS IN BLOCKCHAIN AND CRYPTOCURRENCY

facilitate interoperability between different blockchains will enable seamless integration and communication, fostering a more connected and robust ecosystem.

The future of blockchain and cryptocurrency is undoubtedly bright, with numerous opportunities for innovation and growth. As the technology matures and becomes more widely adopted, it has the potential to transform industries, empower individuals, and create a more transparent and equitable global economy.

7

Chapter 12: Embracing the Blockchain Revolution

As we stand on the brink of a new era, the blockchain revolution presents an unparalleled opportunity to reshape our world in ways we have yet to fully comprehend. The transformative potential of blockchain technology extends far beyond cryptocurrencies, offering the promise of enhanced security, transparency, and efficiency across various sectors.

To harness the full potential of blockchain, it is essential for individuals, businesses, and governments to embrace a forward-thinking mindset and actively explore the possibilities this technology offers. Education and awareness are crucial in this endeavor, as a deeper understanding of blockchain can empower people to make informed decisions and drive innovation.

Collaboration and cooperation will be key to overcoming the challenges and unlocking the opportunities presented by blockchain technology. By fostering a spirit of openness and collaboration, stakeholders can work together to address issues such as scalability, security, and regulatory compliance. This collaborative approach can also lead to the development of new use cases and applications, further expanding the reach and impact of blockchain technology.

As we navigate the complexities of this emerging landscape, it is essential to maintain a focus on ethical considerations and social responsibility. The decentralized nature of blockchain has the potential to democratize access to information and resources, but it also requires careful stewardship to ensure that its benefits are equitably distributed. By prioritizing inclusivity, sustainability, and transparency, we can create a future where blockchain technology serves the greater good.

The journey of blockchain and cryptocurrency is still in its early stages, with many exciting developments and discoveries yet to come. By embracing this revolutionary technology and working together to overcome its challenges, we can unlock a future of endless possibilities and drive meaningful change in our world.

www.ingramcontent.com/pod-product-compliance
Lightning Source LLC
LaVergne TN
LVHW020509080526
838202LV00057B/6257